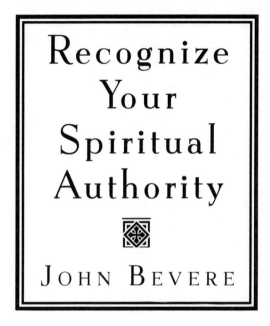

Recognize Your Spiritual Authority

JOHN BEVERE

Charisma
HOUSE
Books about Spirit-Led Living

The Inner Strength Series
LIVING WITH STRENGTH IN TODAY'S WORLD

RECOGNIZE YOUR SPIRITUAL AUTHORITY by John Bevere
Published by Charisma House
A part of Strang Communications Company
600 Rinehart Road
Lake Mary, Florida 32746
www.charismahouse.com

Unless otherwise noted, all Scripture quotations are from the
New King James Version of the Bible. Copyright © 1979, 1980,
1982 by Thomas Nelson, Inc., publishers. Used by permission.

Scripture quotations marked AMP are from the Amplified Bible.
Old Testament copyright © 1965, 1987 by the Zondervan
Corporation. The Amplified New Testament copyright ©
1954, 1958, 1987 by the Lockman Corporation. Used by permission.

Scripture quotations marked NIV are from the Holy Bible, New
International Version. Copyright © 1973, 1978, 1984,
International Bible Society. Used by permission.

Cover design by Rachel Campbell

Library of Congress Catalog Card Number: 2001098127
International Standard Book Number: 0-88419-834-0

02 03 04 05   87654321
Printed in the United States of America

Contents

Introduction

Regardless of your age, economic status, position in the work world, physical condition or social standing, if you have accepted Jesus Christ as your Lord and Savior, you can possess an inner strength that makes you victorious in Christ—and in the destiny God has chosen for your life.

Yet many believers often feel weak, helpless and inadequate to live strong, powerful spiritual lives, yielding to the temptations of the enemy, succumbing to the carnal passions of their human natures and failing to rise up in victory in their spiritual lives. Why does this happen? How does a believer grab hold of that inner strength and live in its power?

This book will help you to understand how important it is to recognize the spiritual position and authority that is yours as a man or woman of God. It will teach you how to resist Satan's intimidating attacks and to overcome the fears that keep you from being a strong, bold, victorious overcomer.

David said, "The LORD is the strength of my life; of whom shall I be afraid?" (Ps. 27:1). David declared the Lord his source of strength and power. David was so confident in God's power that he was able to put his life on the line—again and again—as he faced wild lions, a terrifying giant, enemy armies and even the king he served.

Before David there was another man who showed this great inner strength that can be yours. As a young man, Caleb, along with eleven other Israelite warriors, was sent by Moses to spy out the Promised Land and report to Moses how difficult it would be for the children of Israel to take possession of this land to which God had led them. Ten spies returned with this report: "The land through which we have gone as spies is a land that devours its inhabitants, and all the people whom we saw in it are men of great stature…and we were like grasshoppers in our own sight, and so we were in their sight" (Num. 13:32–33).

These ten men failed to walk in the position of

strength and authority that God had given to them. Only two—Caleb and Joshua—returned with a good report. Upon hearing the ten spies give their bad report, Caleb "quieted the people before Moses, and said, 'Let us go up at once and take possession, for we are well able to overcome it'" (v. 30).

Caleb stands as an overcomer of incredible inner strength in God. But he was young, healthy, physically strong and perhaps speaking out of the brashness of youth! You may not be young, and you may think your strength has passed and left you weak and vulnerable to the enemy's attacks.

But as an eighty-five-year-old man, Caleb still possessed this great inner strength. Forty-five years after the Israelites marched into the Promised Land and took possession, Joshua was dividing the territory among the twelve tribes. When the tribe of Judah stood before Joshua, Caleb also stood bold and strong before him and claimed a special inheritance that Moses had promised to him when they entered the land:

> Then the children of Judah came to Joshua
> in Gilgal. And Caleb the son of Jephunneh

the Kenizzite said to him: "You know the word which the LORD said to Moses the man of God concerning you and me in Kadesh Barnea. I was forty years old when Moses the servant of the LORD sent me from Kadesh Barnea to spy out the land, and I brought back word to him as it was in my heart. Nevertheless my brethren who went up with me made the heart of the people melt, but I wholly followed the LORD my God. So Moses swore on that day, saying, 'Surely the land where your foot has trodden shall be your inheritance and your children's forever, because you have wholly followed the LORD my God.' And now, behold, the LORD has kept me alive, as He said, these forty-five years, ever since the LORD spoke this word to Moses while Israel wandered in the wilderness; and now, here I am this day, eighty-five years old. As yet I am as strong this day as on the day that Moses sent me; just as my strength was then, so now is my strength for war, both for going out and for coming in. Now therefore, give me this mountain of which the LORD spoke in that day; for you heard in that day how the Anakim were there, and that the cities were great and fortified. It may be that the LORD will be with me, and I shall be able to drive them out as the LORD said."

—JOSHUA 14:6–12

Wouldn't you like to get to your eighty-fifth year and be able to say, "I am as strong this day as on the day God saved me"? You can be! You can be even stronger! By learning to recognize your spiritual position and authority in Christ, resisting the devil and using the spiritual tools and gifts God imparts to you as a man or woman of God, you can be a Caleb of today.

Keep reading! The confidence and strength that David and Caleb possessed is available to you. Why? Because of Jesus. No name is higher; no power is greater. In His words, "Behold! I have given you authority and power…over all the power that the enemy [possesses]; and nothing shall in any way harm you" (Luke 10:19, AMP).

Rise up, mighty man and woman of God. Possess this great inner strength that is yours. Step into your spiritual position in Christ. Live in the authority that God has given to you.

ONE

Resist Spiritual Intimidation

DEVELOPING
Inner Strength

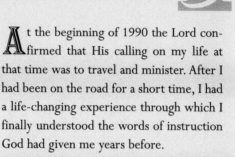

At the beginning of 1990 the Lord confirmed that His calling on my life at that time was to travel and minister. After I had been on the road for a short time, I had a life-changing experience through which I finally understood the words of instruction God had given me years before.

We had begun conducting the meetings at a church on a Wednesday evening and were scheduled to continue through Sunday. The Spirit of God moved in a very powerful way, and there were strong deliverances, healings and salvation. The presence of God in the meetings grew each night.

The first week a lady involved in the New Age movement was gloriously delivered. This seemed to be the catalyst that spurred the meetings on. Within a week people were coming from a ninety-mile radius.

The pastor said, "We can't stop these

meetings. God has more in store for us." I agreed, and we continued for twenty-one services. The Word of God flowed like a swift-running brook, and the gifts of the Spirit manifested in every service.

During the second week of the meetings, one night I turned around as I was preaching and faced the musicians and singers (there were about twenty-five on the platform). Then I declared, "There is sin on this platform. If you do not repent, God will expose it."

After hearing myself say that, I thought, *Wow, where did that come from?* I had been preaching long enough to know there are times when God's anointing on you is so strong that you will make statements that your physical ears will hear only after they're already said. This is prophetic preaching—when we speak by divine inspiration.

My mind began to question what I said, but I quickly dismissed those thoughts because I knew what I said was from God. I had not premeditated it. The anointing to preach remained heavily upon me.

The crowds grew at each service. During the third week—again, as I preached—I wheeled around, pointed my finger at those on the platform and declared boldly through the unction of the Holy Spirit, "There is sin on this platform. If you do not repent, God will expose it, and you will be removed!" I sensed an increase in authority and assurance. This time I did not question it because I knew God was in the process of purging sin from His house.

I f sin creeps into our lives, the Holy Spirit convicts and instructs us. However, if we do not listen, we will begin to grow cold and dull. This will continue until we are no longer sensitive to Him in our hearts.

Then, in order to reach and protect us or those around us, God will send someone to expose what is wrong. He does not do this for the purpose of embarrassing us, but to warn and protect us. If we still refuse to listen, judgment comes. "For if we would judge ourselves, we would not be judged. But when we are judged, we are chastened by the Lord, that we may not be condemned with the world" (1 Cor. 11:31–32).

God will tolerate sin for a season to give us time to repent in order to spare us His chastening. Even in His chastening it is His desire that we would not be condemned along with the world. The prodigal son came to his senses when he was in the pigpen. Better to come to your senses in a pigpen than to continue in your sin and one day hear the Master say, "Depart from Me, you who practice lawlessness!" (Matt. 7:23).

If we do not repent, we suffer even though that is not God's desire for us. Referring to this, Paul said, "For this reason many are weak and sick among you, and many sleep [are dead]" (1 Cor. 11:30). Sin eventually brings forth spiritual and physical death. I felt that the Lord was chastening someone on the platform, trying to bring that person to repentance. But I did not know whom He was convicting of sin.

> If we do not repent, we suffer
> even though that is not
> God's desire for us.

A Challenge of Authority

The evening after I stood on that platform and warned the people standing with me of God's coming judgment, the pastor and I were in his office preparing to go out to the service. An elder came in and reported that the ministers of music and praise seemed moody and negative that night. The pastor thought they were just tired from so many services and said, "Just tell them to go out and praise God and put their feelings aside."

I looked at the elder and said, "Wait a minute. Is there something wrong?"

The elder answered, "Well, they think you are being too hard on them. They feel that you should address them privately rather than publicly."

Although I was unaware of it at the time, this was a very crucial moment. My God-given authority to serve and protect was being challenged. The enemy was not pleased with what was happening in these meetings, and he wanted to put a stop to it.

I had a choice, although at that time I was not aware of it. I could yield to the intimidation by backing down on what I had said to the ministers of music, thereby forfeiting my position of authority. Or I could stay in my authority, breaking the power of their intimidation by staying strong in what God had said.

Immediately I thought, *John, why did you embarrass those people? Why couldn't you just preach your message without turning around and pointing fingers? Now the people in the church are busy trying to figure out who on the platform is in sin. What if no one is? Or even if there is sin, what if it's never exposed? People will still be suspicious, and those who are pure will suffer. The church will be hindered. Have I destroyed the good that has been done in this church? If I have, it will give me a bad reputation, and I've only just started to travel.*

On and on these thoughts assaulted my mind. My fears had begun to center on one thought: What is going to happen to me? This is how intimidation will change your focus. The reason: The root of intimidation is fear, and fear causes people to focus on themselves. Perfect love casts out fear because love puts the focus on God and others and denies itself (1 John 4:18).

The pastor said nothing. The three of us grabbed hands and prayed that God's will would be done in that service. We proceeded out to the platform just as we had each night for the past three weeks. During the praise and worship I noticed the word of the Lord was not filling my heart. I felt no direction, but I thought, *God is faithful. I'll know what to say and do by the time I get to the pulpit.*

Praise and worship was over, and as the pastor made announcements, I heard nothing in my heart. I thought, *I'll get up and God will give me direction as I stand on my feet.* I am not one who prepares outlines and has sermons ready. I study, pray and then speak from my heart by inspiration. My concern grew as the time passed because I knew I had nothing to say if God did not give me His direction.

> # The root of intimidation is fear, and fear causes people to focus on themselves.

Then the pastor introduced me. I came to the pulpit, and because I had no direction, I said, "Let's pray." But as we prayed, I still received no direction. I prayed for several minutes. To make matters worse my prayers were lifeless. It was as if my words were coming out of my mouth only to fall at my feet. I thought, *What am I going to do?* I resolved to deliver a message out of the Psalms that I had preached before.

As I preached, I sensed no life, no anointing on the message. I struggled to keep my thoughts together. God seemed nowhere to be found. I would think, *Why did I just say that?* or, *Where am I taking this?* It was as if I were being led by confusion, not by the Holy Spirit. I kept consoling myself that God would show up and salvage the mess I was in. However, it just got worse. I finally ended the message and the service after about thirty-five minutes.

Baffled, I went back to the place where I was staying. "God, why didn't You show up?" I asked. "Every service has been wonderful and powerful, yet this service had no life. If I were the people, I wouldn't come back. As a matter of fact, *I* don't want to go back." That night I went to bed feeling as if I'd swallowed a sack of sand.

The next morning I woke up feeling as if the sack of sand had grown into a pile. I felt so heavy that I didn't want to get out of bed. Joy eluded me. I went out to pray. I asked God again, "Why didn't You show up?"

No response.

"Have I sinned? Did I grieve You?"

Still silence. I prayed for an hour, and every minute was a struggle.

I put on a praise tape and began to sing along. I reasoned, *God gives the garment of praise for the spirit of heaviness. I have got to get rid of this.* However, I only experienced a half hour of lifeless singing. I became more frustrated. "What have I done? Why won't You answer me?"

After lunch I went out to a nearby field. I thought, *I'll bind the devil. That will do it.* But I was the only one who felt bound. I was out praying and yelling at the devil for three hours and almost lost my voice. I had to go in and get ready for the service. I consoled myself, *With all this resistance, tonight God will show up strong, John; just walk by faith.*

We went through the praise, worship, announcements and offering that night, and I felt the same foreboding I had the night before. Again I reasoned, *God will come through as soon as I get up there.* I was introduced and again—nothing. I prayed for direction, and there was silence.

I began to preach another message I had ministered before and was overwhelmed with confusion. There was no life, direction or anointing. After five minutes of this mess I said, "Folks, we need to pray. Something is just not right!" The entire congregation stood up, and we all began to pray fervently.

Intimidation Exposed

All of a sudden I heard the voice of God speak to me for the first time in more than twenty-four hours. He said, "John, you are intimidated by those people on the platform behind you. You've been knocked out of your position of authority, and the gift of God in you has been quenched."

With this gentle rebuke a burst of light flooded my spirit. While everyone prayed for the next five minutes, the Spirit of God walked me through the Bible, showing me numerous incidents when men and women were intimidated and how this caused the gift of God in them to go dormant. I saw how they yielded their authority and lost their effectiveness in the Spirit. Then He walked me through the past several years and showed me how I'd done the same.

I immediately began breaking the power of intimidation off myself through prayer. For the next seventy-five minutes I preached from the Scriptures God had given me like a man on fire. When I finished, two-thirds of the congregation came forward to receive freedom from intimidation. That was the greatest service of the entire revival.

Less than a week later God started to expose the sin on the platform. It was discovered that the bass player was going out after services and getting drunk. In addition, one of the singers was sleeping with a young girl in the congregation. They were both removed from their ministry positions. The bass player left the church, but the singer repented and was restored in his walk with the Lord.

A short time later the praise and worship leader and a few others caused a split in the church. A fourth of the church left with them. As it turned out, the praise and worship leader was involved in adultery, and within a year she divorced her husband. At last report she was living with another man. Out of the families that led the split, only one couple is still married.

These were the people who had complained that I was too hard on them. God was giving them a warning. How much better it would have been if only they had taken that warning to heart.

I have returned to this church twice and discovered more unity and strength there than ever before. The pastor explained, "It was God purging our church, and it has made us stronger. Our praise and worship has never been so free!" He also said a lot of the contention and strife he'd previously dealt with was no longer there. Praise God!

A Message for All

Although this message was revealed as I sought God in the midst of a ministry conflict, do not think its lesson is limited to those who stand behind a pulpit. Countless Christians battle intimidation. Often those who are intimidated don't realize what they're fighting. As with most of Satan's devices, intimidation is camouflaged and subtle. We feel its effects—depression, confusion, lack of faith—without knowing its root. Had I realized I was intimidated, I would not have had such a struggle at that church. But I thank God for the lesson it taught me.

In frustration most of us deal with the aftermath, or fruit, of intimidation rather than with intimidation itself—and with its root. Therefore, we may experience temporary relief, but our struggles do not end. You can pick all the fruit off a tree, but as long as its roots are intact, the fruit eventually grows back. This cycle can be discouraging because we feel as though we just cannot rid ourselves of these hindrances. We begin to feel hopeless and settle for a place far below where God has called us.

> You can pick all the fruit off a tree, but as long as its roots are intact, the fruit eventually grows back.

The truths in this book will equip you with the knowledge you need to recognize the powerful inner strength you possess to fulfill your call as a servant of our Lord Jesus Christ. Like David and Caleb—and like Jesus Himself, the strong Son of God—you can be victorious and live in the fullness of the destiny God has for your life. Begin by recognizing your position and authority in Christ.

Adapted from John Bevere, *Breaking Intimidation* (Lake Mary, FL: Charisma House, 1995), 14–21.

TWO

Walk in Your God-Given Authority

DEVELOPING
Inner Strength

As I serve the Lord, I realize more and more that He uses circumstances and people to prepare us to fulfill His calling for our lives.

In 1983 I left my career position as an engineer to enter the full-time ministry of helps for a very large church. In my position I served the pastor, his wife and all incoming guest ministers by taking care of menial tasks in order to free them up for the work God called them to do. After four years God released me to be the youth pastor for another large church.

The week I was to leave, a man who was also on staff told my wife that God had given him a word for me. Ever since then that word has resounded in my ear as a warning, offering protection in the shadow of its wisdom and strength. As with any true word of God, it has become a rudder for my heart and a foundation to keep me from uncertainty.

This man warned my wife, "If John does not walk in his God-given authority, someone will take it from him and use it against him." This word had an immediate impact. I recognized it as the wisdom of God, but I did not have the full understanding of how to apply it. That knowledge would come over the next several years.

What does it mean to "walk in your God-given authority"? When God spoke those words through the prophetic word that was given to me, I wasn't really sure what He meant—or how I was to respond to His word to me. The prophetic word came as a warning: "If you don't walk in your God-given authority, someone will take it from you and use it against you."

It is important to understand there is a dwelling place or position in the spirit that we hold as believers in Jesus. With this position comes authority. This authority is what the enemy wants. If he can get us to yield our God-given authority, he will take it and use it against us. This affects not only us but also those entrusted to our care.

There are several scriptures pertaining to our place of authority in the spirit. Let's examine a few.

> He who dwells in the secret place of the Most High shall abide under the shadow of the Almighty.
>
> —Psalm 91:1

> He also brought me out into a broad place;

He delivered me because He delighted in me.

—Psalm 18:19

My foot stands in an even place; in the congregations I will bless the Lord.

—Psalm 26:12

Believers literally occupy a *place* in the spirit. It is imperative that you as a believer not only know that place but also function in it. If you do not know your position, you cannot function properly in the body of Christ.

This position and the authority it carries can be lost or stolen. A clear biblical example is Judas Iscariot. After Jesus ascended to heaven, the disciples gathered to pray. At that time, Peter explained what had happened to Judas:

For it is written in the Book of Psalms: "Let his dwelling place be desolate, and let no one live in it."

—Acts 1:20

Judas permanently lost his place in the spirit by transgression (Acts 1:16–17). This is the primary way the enemy knocks people out of their spiritual authority. It is how he caused Adam and Eve to fall, consequently displacing them and gaining lordship over them and all they ruled.

Adam and Eve held the highest position of authority on the earth. Every living creature and all of nature were under their authority. God said, "Let them have dominion over the fish of the sea, over the birds of the air, and over the cattle, over all the earth and over every creeping thing that creeps on the earth" (Gen. 1:26). Nothing on this earth in the spiritual or natural realms was above the authority of mankind—only God Himself.

> **If you do not know your position, you cannot function properly in the body of Christ.**

When Adam held his position of authority, there was no disease, earthquakes, famine or poverty. It was the dominion of heaven on this earth as Adam walked in fellowship with God and ruled by God's delegated authority and power. But with the sin of

Adam came the demise of everything underneath his authority. By transgression he yielded his place in the spirit to the enemy of God.

The Scriptures bear testimony to this by Satan's boast as he tempted Jesus in the wilderness. Satan took Him on a high mountain to show Him all the kingdoms of the world, declaring:

> All this authority I will give You, and their glory; for this has been delivered to me, and I give it to whomever I wish.
>
> —LUKE 4:6

God had entrusted authority to Adam, and Adam in turn forfeited it to Satan. Adam lost more than just his position. All that God had placed under his care was affected. A gradual decline of all harmony and order took place.

One example is in the animal kingdom. In the garden, under God and Adam's domain, lions did not devour the other animals, cobras did not have venomous bites, and lambs had no reason to fear wolves or other creatures of prey (Isa. 65:25). Yet, immediately after the Fall we see an innocent animal sacrificed to clothe the naked man (Gen. 3:21). Later we see enmity and fear placed between man and the animals that he once ruled over (Gen. 9:2).

Another area affected was the earth itself. The ground became cursed, working against man instead of for him as he toiled to bring forth the fruit that once had been bountifully provided (Gen. 3:17–19). Romans 8:20 tells us, "For the creation was subjected to futility, not willingly."

Nothing on earth, whether natural or spiritual, escaped the effects of disobedience. Iniquity, death, disease, poverty, earthquakes, famines, pestilence and more entered the earth. There was a loss of divine order and authority. Adam's firstborn learned to hate, envy and murder. The enemy had taken the authority God had given for protection and provision and turned it against all creation, using it now for destruction and death.

Restored Authority

A man forfeited his position of authority; therefore, only a man could restore it. Thousands of years later Jesus was born. His mother was a daughter of God's covenant people; His Father, the Holy Spirit of God. He was not part man and part God. He was *Immanuel*, "God with us," or "God revealed in a man" (Matt. 1:23). The fact that He was human gave Him the legal right to regain what was lost. As the Son of God, He was free from the lordship Satan had acquired over man.

> # Jesus, through obedience and sacrifice, restored the God-given authority Adam had lost.

He revealed the will of God in everything. Sins were forgiven because in His presence sin had no dominion. Sickness and disease bowed to His authority and power (Luke 5:20–24). Nature itself was subjected to His command (Mark 4:39). He walked in the authority that Adam had relinquished. Jesus, through obedience and sacrifice, restored the God-given authority Adam had lost, and therefore, our relationship with God.

Before He returned to His Father, Jesus declared, "All authority has been given to Me in heaven and on earth. Go therefore and make disciples of all the nations, baptizing them in the name of the Father and of the Son and of the Holy Spirit, teaching them to observe all things that I have commanded you; and lo, I am with you always, even to the end of the age" (Matt. 28:18–20).

It is clear that Jesus regained what Adam lost and more. Satan and Adam only had dominion over the earth, but Jesus' dominion included not only the earth but also heaven. Jesus had risen above the place of authority Satan had dispossessed. After revealing His position and authority, Jesus told us to "go therefore." Why did Jesus make this connection between His authority and our calling? We find the answer in the writings of the apostle Paul.

Positions of Authority

Paul prayed we would know "what is the exceeding greatness of His power toward us who believe… which He worked in Christ when He raised Him from the dead and seated Him at His right hand in the heavenly *places*" (Eph. 1:19–20, emphasis added). Notice it is not a singular heavenly place; Paul clearly says "places." The reason for this is found a few verses later as we read, "And you He made alive, who were dead in trespasses and sins...and raised us up together, and made us sit together in the heavenly *places* in Christ Jesus" (Eph. 2:1, 6, emphasis added). These *places* are where His redeemed children are to dwell.

> If Satan can steal or cause individuals to lay down their position of authority, then he once again has authority to operate.

Now the question, Where are these dwelling places, and what position do they hold? The answer is found in Ephesians 1:21: "...far *above* all principality and power and might and dominion, and every name that is named, not only in this age but also in that which is to come" (emphasis added).

A redeemed man hidden in Christ is now given a position in the Spirit above the devil. Jesus boldly declared, "Behold, I give you the authority...over all the power of the enemy, and nothing shall by any means hurt you" (Luke 10:19).

Now we understand the command, "Go therefore." Jesus understood the authority He was entrusting to believers. Our rebirth rights have positioned us in those heavenly places far above the enemy's authority and power.

Just as he did with Adam in the Garden of Eden, Satan now seeks to displace us in the spirit in order to regain the authority Jesus stripped from him. If Satan can steal or cause individuals to lay down their position of authority, then he once again has authority to operate. Paul says so clearly, "[Do not] give *place* to the devil" (Eph. 4:27, emphasis added). We believers must not forfeit our place in the spirit.

Rank in the Kingdom

We must realize the kingdom of God is just that— a *kingdom.* Kingdoms are structured by rank and authority. Heaven's domain is no exception. The higher the rank, the more influence and authority.

In the garden, Satan wasn't after the animals. He understood authority and went after God's man. He knew if he got the man, he would possess all that the man ruled over and cared for.

So when the enemy goes after a church, his primary target is the leadership. Recently a pastor of a large congregation decided to divorce his wife. There was no scriptural reason for this, and it devastated his wife and children. When the leadership under him questioned his motive, he told them if they didn't like it they could leave.

> # When Satan knocks the keeper of a house out of his position, all those under his care are vulnerable.

He willfully transgressed the commandment of God, releasing a spirit of divorce and deception throughout his congregation. After this, there was an increase of divorce in his church, even among leadership. Others became discouraged. Shell-shocked, they drifted from church to church, wondering whom they could trust. When Satan knocks the *keeper of a house* out of his position, all those under his care are vulnerable.

I have watched as parents willfully transgress the commandments of God. It is then only a matter of time before their children follow their example. You may call it a curse, but why does it happen? Through sin parents have forfeited their position of authority in the spirit, leaving their children vulnerable to the enemy.

Giving Occasion to the Enemies of the Lord

This principle is illustrated in the life of David (2 Sam. 8–18). The kingdom was strong and secure under his leadership. God had blessed him with several sons and daughters. Then David took for himself what God had not given him—he committed adultery with Bathsheba. She became pregnant, and to complicate matters, her husband was away at war defending David's realm.

David sent for her husband, Uriah, hoping to encourage him to sleep with Bathsheba and therefore appear to have fathered the baby. However, Uriah, in devotion to David and his kingdom, would not enjoy intimacy with his wife while his fellow soldiers were in combat. David saw that the plan to cover his sin was not going to work. He knew it would only be a matter of time before Uriah learned his wife was pregnant. Eventually everyone would know the father was David.

So David planned Uriah's murder, sending him back to the battle carrying his own death warrant. Uriah was put amid the fiercest fighting. Then, when he was surrounded by the enemy, those fighting beside him were ordered to draw back. Uriah fell by the enemy's hand. David's one act of adultery led to deceit, lying and murder.

Soon the prophet Nathan came to David to expose this sin. David confessed, "I have sinned against the LORD." Then Nathan said to David, "The LORD also has put away your sin; you shall not die" (2 Sam. 12:13).

David repented and was forgiven. God released him from his transgression (Isa. 43:25–26). But Nathan goes on to warn David: "By this deed you have given great occasion to the enemies of the LORD" (2 Sam. 12:14).

David was forgiven, but he had made his life and family vulnerable to the enemies of God—not only natural enemies but also spiritual ones. His family and the nation of Israel suffered greatly.

David's first child by Bathsheba died. David's oldest son, Amnon, heir to the throne, raped his half-sister, Tamar. Absalom, son of David and brother of Tamar, took revenge and killed his half-brother Amnon.

Absalom turned the hearts of many of the men of Israel against David and took his throne. He defiled his father's concubines and sent the men of Israel out to hunt down and kill David. The plot failed, and Absalom was killed.

Three of David's sons died because he had exposed his family to the enemies of God by his transgression.

I have seen ministers' children who are on drugs, hostile to church and bound to lust and homosexuality because their parents forfeited their positions in the spirit through transgression. We need to take the Bible seriously when it says, "Not many of you should presume to be teachers, my brothers, because you know that we who teach will be judged more strictly" (James 3:1, NIV). The reason teachers (pastors) are judged more strictly is because of the great impact of their disobedience. They not only hurt themselves but all those placed under their guardianship as well. God forgives them just as He did David. However, they will still reap what they sow. The enemy is given *place!*

I realize these are hard words. I appeal to you with all humility and write these words with fear and trembling. We have seen too many tragedies, especially in ministries. We must not judge or condemn. We need to forgive and reach out to those who have failed. If they repent, they will be forgiven by God. But I write these words as instruction and warning to those the enemy will target. We all must walk in humility and restoration.

I have four sons. I have come to realize the awesome responsibility and accountability I have for their lives. They are God's, and I am just a steward placed over them. I never want to see their lives devastated because I gave place to the devil.

When I was in the ministry of serving, I took care of menial things so those I served could go about fulfilling God's call on their lives. I took care of the dry cleaning, picked up their children from school, washed their cars and so on. One day God spoke something to me that gave me a sobering outlook on the ministry. He said, "Son, if you mess up in this position, it can be easily corrected because you're dealing with natural things. But when I place you in a ministry position, you are over people, and lives are at stake."

Relinquishing Authority

This chapter gave you an understanding of spiritual position and authority. We have seen examples of several people who lost or gave up their authority to the enemy of God. Satan will blatantly try to steal your authority by bringing sin into your life. As you determine to serve God by exhibiting that inner strength from Him, Satan will try to knock you out of your position in Christ through intimidation. Rise up like Caleb and tell the devil, "Give me this mountain of which the Lord spoke. It belongs to me—not to you!"

Adapted from *Breaking Intimidation*, 13–14, 23–31.

THREE

Avoid Two Detrimental Extremes

DEVELOPING
Inner Strength

I used to pray, "God, use me to win the lost. Use me to heal multitudes and deliver the masses." I would pray this over and over, and that was the extent of my seeking after God. My highest goal was to be a successful minister.

Then one day Jesus showed me that my emphasis was off. He shocked me by saying, "John, Judas cast out devils, healed the sick and preached the gospel. He left his business to become My disciple, but where is he today?" This hit me like a ton of bricks! He continued, "The goal of the high call of Christianity is not the power of God or ministry; it is to know Me." (See Philippians 3:10–15.)

Later, as my wife prayed to be used along these same lines, Jesus questioned her, "Lisa, have you ever been used by a friend?"

"Yes," she answered.

"How did you feel?"

She answered, "I felt betrayed!"

Jesus went on to say, "Lisa, I don't use people. I anoint, heal, transform and conform them to My image, but I don't use them."

In just a few moments the Spirit of God can drop a wealth of insight into your spirit. But that revelation is of no value without the wisdom and character to live it out.

When the Holy Spirit led me through the Scriptures about confronting intimidation, He showed me two extremes that will throw a believer's life out of balance: The first extreme is pursuing power; the second is false humility. The proper balance is found in the life of Timothy, who cultivated godly character rather than false humility and stirred up his gift rather than pursue power.

A Pure Heart

It was in Lystra that the apostle Paul first met Timothy, a young man whose mother was a Christian Jew and whose father was Greek.

Paul wanted Timothy to accompany him and Silas as their traveling assistant. Timothy would be responsible to care for the needs of Paul (Acts 19:22).

As time went by, Timothy's faithfulness as a servant was proved. He was promoted and entrusted as a minister of the gospel, eventually pastoring the church in Ephesus. In his second letter to Timothy Paul wrote:

> I call to remembrance the genuine faith that is in you, which dwelt first in your grandmother Lois and your mother Eunice, and I am persuaded is in you also. Therefore I remind you to stir up the gift of God.
>
> —2 Timothy 1:5–6

Notice Paul references the fact that Timothy's faith was genuine. This young man's heart was pure. He was not a charlatan. In another letter Paul commends, "But I trust in the Lord Jesus to send Timothy to you shortly…for I have no one like-minded, who will sincerely care for your state. For all seek their own, not the things which are of Christ Jesus. But you know his proven character, that as a son with his father he served with me in the gospel" (Phil. 2:19–22).

It is clear that Timothy's character was not in question. As Christians, character should be our first priority and pursuit. What our Father looks for is not power, but character. It is a sad fact that many in the church pursue the power and

---

anointing of the Spirit while sidestepping the pursuit of godly character. First Corinthians 14:1 instructs us to "pursue love, and desire spiritual gifts." However, we have perverted that command. We *pursue* the gifts and the anointing and just *wish* for the fruit of love in our lives. God is love, and until we walk in love we will not attain His nature.

> As Christians, character should be our first priority and pursuit.

One Extreme: Pursuing Power Rather Than Character

Some Christians will travel great distances— hundreds of miles—to go to a miracle, prophetic or anointing service, but they are unwilling to deal with the anger, unforgiveness or bitterness in their own hearts. This is evidence that their emphasis is on power rather than character.

The spiritual manifestations at these services

may be of God, but we have to deal with the inner man, too. This unwillingness to deal with the inward has opened up many to deception. Even though the church is experiencing a refreshing at this time, sin must be dealt with. It is wonderful that people are so hungry for the power of God, but let's not neglect purity of heart.

We have seen too many ministers fall. But they didn't fall when they committed their first act of immorality. No, they began to fall earlier—the day success in ministry became more important than their intimate relationship with God. We've not only seen this among ministers, but also within their congregations.

Jesus said, "Blessed are the pure in heart, for they shall see God" (Matt. 5:8). He did not say, "Blessed are those who have a successful ministry." He said that without a pure heart you will not see God! Of course, Jesus is the only one who can give us a pure heart. It is not something we can earn. It is both priceless and free—priceless in that it required the death of God's Son, and free in that it is given without cost to all who will seek Him.

Paul's sole ambition was to know Him (Phil.

3:8–10). Moses said, "Show me now Your way, that I may know You" (Exod. 33:13). David cried, "One thing I have desired of the LORD, that will I seek: that I may dwell in the house of the LORD all the days of my life, to behold the beauty of the LORD, and to inquire in His temple" (Ps. 27:4). And again, "My soul thirsts for You; my flesh longs for You" (Ps. 63:1).

The anointing of God is not His approval.

The men and women of the Bible who desired to know God more than anything else stayed faithful to Him, finishing the course He set before them. They learned the secret of integrity with power. Seeking Him earnestly, they glimpsed His very heart.

Some people gauge their spiritual maturity by their ability to prophesy or flow in the gifts. Yet remember, gifts are given, not earned. A donkey spoke and saw into the realm of the spirit. A rooster crowed three times and convicted Peter. Does that make these beasts spiritual?

Jesus said that many would call Him Lord and expect entrance into His kingdom, only to be denied. They will have done miracles, cast out devils and prophesied in His name. But He will answer, "Depart from Me, you who practice lawlessness!" (Matt. 7:23).

The anointing of God is not His approval. Saul prophesied after God had rejected him (1 Sam. 19:23–24). Caiaphas prophesied while his one goal was to kill God's Son (John 11:49–51). We must have God's heart to be able to obey His will. Without it we will walk in merely a shadow of His anointing, troubled by legalism or lasciviousness. Balaam prophesied, and his prophecies proved true; however, he died the death of a soothsayer, put to the sword when Israel invaded the Promised Land.

Paul measured Timothy's virtues by the purity of his heart and the faithfulness of his service. We must also set this standard before us and allow the Holy Spirit to accurately weigh us. This extremely important prerequisite cannot be overemphasized as we go into battle with the spirit of intimidation. Without this undergirding, the truth in this message will not set you free and could possibly do you more damage than good. For it is not the words themselves that carry the power to liberate, but it is the spirit and substance behind them.

To explain this, we recall what Peter warned: "As also our beloved brother Paul, according to the wisdom given to him, has written to you, as also in all his epistles, speaking in them of these things, in which are some things hard to understand, which untaught and unstable people twist to their own destruction, as they do also the rest of the Scriptures" (2 Pet. 3:15–16).

It is not the words themselves that carry the power to liberate, but it is the spirit and substance behind them.

It is more important that we pursue a right relationship with God than a formula to move in His power. In light of this, examine Paul's opening statements in 2 Timothy. After establishing Timothy's pureness of heart, Paul wrote, "Therefore I remind you to stir up the gift of God" (2 Tim. 1:6). The word *therefore* means "for that reason." So Paul's instructions to Timothy concerning the release of the gift of God in Timothy's life would be invalid if his faith was not genuine. Now let's continue.

The Other Extreme: False Humility

> ... when I call to remembrance the genuine faith that is in you, which dwelt first in your grandmother Lois and your mother Eunice, and I am persuaded is in you also. Therefore I remind you to stir up the gift of God which is in you through the laying on of my hands.
>
> —2 TIMOTHY 1:5–6

"Therefore I remind you." Paul was referring to his first letter to Timothy in which he exhorted, "Do not neglect the gift that is in you, which was given to you by prophecy with the laying on of the hands of the eldership" (1 Tim. 4:14). Paul stressed to Timothy the importance of not neglecting the gift of God by writing about it a second time and by making it one of the first things he mentioned in the letter.

To elaborate on what it means not to neglect the gift, let's look at some antonyms. The opposite of *neglect* is to:

> Accomplish, achieve, act, attend, care for, complete, conclude, consider, consummate.

All of these are words of action and authority. Most words have both a verb and a noun form. They are positive and decisive. To further rightly divide the word of God, let's examine what it means to neglect:

> Breach, disdain, dismiss, disregard, discount, ignore, underestimate, overlook, undervalue, scorn, despise.

These are all negative words signifying a lack of action, decisiveness and authority. It is a serious and weighty thing to neglect what is entrusted to us. We suffer loss when we neglect.

The opposite extreme of simply pursuing the power is living in what I describe as a state of false humility. People living in such a state recognize the importance of pursuing God's character, but they stop there. They never venture out into God's gifting in their lives because they are afraid. They avoid anything that involves confrontation, perceiving it as a lack of love or Christian character.

I refer to these people as "peacekeepers." At first glance peacekeeping may look appealing, but Jesus never said, "Blessed are the peacekeepers." Rather, He said, "Blessed are the peacemakers, for they shall be called sons of God" (Matt. 5:9). A *peacekeeper* avoids confrontation at any cost. He will go to any length to preserve a false sense of security for himself, which he mistakes for peace.

A *peacemaker*, on the other hand, will boldly confront no matter what it may cost him because he does not worry about himself. Instead, he is motivated by his love for God and truth. Only under these conditions can true peace thrive.

There is peace in the kingdom of God (Rom. 14:17). However, this peace does not come by the absence of confrontation. As Jesus pointed out, "The kingdom of heaven suffers violence, and the violent take it by force" (Matt. 11:12). There is violent opposition to the advancement of God's kingdom.

Often we think, *I'll just ignore this, and it will go away.* But we need to wake up and realize that what we do not confront will not change! This is why Jude urges on the saints with the following:

> Beloved, while I was very diligent to write to you concerning our common salvation, I found it necessary to write to you exhorting you to contend earnestly for the faith which was once for all delivered to the saints.
>
> —JUDE 3

Notice he said "contend earnestly," not hope for the best. *Contend* means "to fight or wage battle." Christianity is not an easy lifestyle! There is constant opposition and resistance to our pursuit of God in both the natural and the spiritual realms!

Paul strengthened Timothy with, "You therefore must endure hardship as a good soldier of Jesus Christ. No one engaged in warfare entangles himself…" (2 Tim. 2:3–4). We are engaged in warfare. We are to have the attitude of a soldier. We are not to back down from evil, but we are to overcome it with good by God's grace (Rom. 12:21).

The letters from Paul were Timothy's marching

orders as he pastored at Ephesus. Timothy faced challenges. There was false doctrine to be exposed, strife and contention to be stopped and leaders to be raised up so that a strong and mature church could develop. And these were just a few of the more obvious responsibilities he must have faced.

> We are not to back down
> from evil, but we are to
> overcome it with good
> by God's grace.

I'm sure there were many opportunities for confrontation. I'm sure accusation and slander were hurled against him by those within the church who were immature or wicked. Besides all this, he had another obstacle to overcome—his age. He was a young man in a church where many were older. This by itself could open a door to intimidation. But in the face of all this, Paul instructed Timothy to remain strong, not forgetting what had been imparted to him. Paul constantly reminded

Timothy to stand in his God-given authority. Perhaps Timothy had backed down at one time, so Paul instructed:

> These things command and teach.
>
> —1 Timothy 4:11

> And these things command, that they may be blameless.
>
> —1 Timothy 5:7

> You therefore, my son, be strong in the grace that is in Christ Jesus.
>
> —2 Timothy 2:1

Maybe Timothy was like so many others today who love God but avoid confrontation. Fear of confrontation makes you easy prey for intimidation.

If you identify with this fear, then this message is sent to bring you courage and liberty. God wants you operating in your inner strength power source to do and be whatever He asks of you. When you are intimidated, there is no joy. And without joy there is no strength. Where there is fear, there is no peace. But as you break out of what has held you back, you'll find joy and peace in abundance!

Adapted from *Breaking Intimidation,* 33–41.

FOUR

Use Your Imparted Gifts

DEVELOPING
Inner Strength

Recall the parable of the talents. The master delivered "to one... five talents, to another two, and to another one, to each according to his own ability" (Matt. 25:15). He then went away on a journey. The first two men used their talents wisely, bringing increase, while the third man buried his.

When the master returned, the first two gave an account of what was done with the talents entrusted to them. The master commended each of them, "Well done, good and faithful servant."

Then the third man came to give account. In fear he had hidden his talent. He perceived his master as unfair, as one who expected too much. So this servant felt justified in his neglect, selfishness and carelessness. Essentially, he told his master, "Look, you have what is yours."

When the master saw how this servant despised what was committed to his care, he called him wicked and lazy. His one talent was taken away and given to the man who had doubled his. Then the unprofitable servant was cast out (Matt. 25:16–30).

We will give an account for the gifts entrusted to us, as all stewards give account of their stewardship. Another word for gift is *ability,* which is defined as "capability, faculty, genius or power." In other words, talent. From this parable we see a vivid illustration of the importance of nurturing and developing the gift, ability or talent with which God has trusted us.

You may be wondering if you have a spiritual position and authority if you are not currently involved in a leadership function or in full-time ministry. You may be asking, "How does this apply to me?" You may think that God imparts His gifts, abilities and talents only to those in leadership. But God gifts each believer with the giftings that believer will need to reach the destiny God has for him.

God gives a place, or position, in the Spirit to each believer. Remember, Paul explained that God has "raised us up together, and made us sit together in the heavenly places in Christ Jesus" (Eph. 2:6). This is where the redeemed children of God are to dwell. Its location is "far above all principality and power and might and dominion, and every name that is named, not only in this age but also in that which is to come. And He put all things under His feet, and gave Him [the Lord Jesus] to be head over all things to the church, which is His body" (Eph. 1:21–23).

The church is the body of Christ. Just as our physical bodies contain many parts that differ in function and ability, even so the members of the body of Christ function in different callings and gifts. God determines their purpose and function. Each is important, and none is independent from the others.

The members of the body of Christ function in different callings and gifts.

Paul declared that all demonic spirits were placed under the feet of Jesus. This clearly illustrates that no devil should exercise authority over a believer. If you are the foot of the body of Christ, the demons are still under you. Jesus said, "Behold, I give you the authority…over all the power of the enemy, and nothing shall by any means hurt you" (Luke 10:19). However, if we don't exercise or walk in our God-given authority, someone will take it from us and use it against us! The enemy is after our position in the spirit.

Gifted to Function

Let's continue in our study of Paul's letter to Timothy.

> Therefore I remind you to stir up the gift of
> God which is in you through the laying on
> of my hands.
>
> —2 TIMOTHY 1:6

The Greek word for gift is *charisma*. Strong's concordance defines the word as "a spiritual endowment." Another definition, adapted from Vine's dictionary, would be "a gift of grace endowed upon believers by the operation of the Holy Spirit." So the word *charisma* describes those spiritual abilities with which God equips believers.

Nothing in the realm of the spirit is accomplished without this *charisma,* or supernatural ability of God. We should not preach, sing, prophesy, lead or even serve without it. There is no life produced without this grace. Lifeless religion is born out of man's attempt to serve God his own way, in his own ability. When we minister to others without the gifting of God, we labor in vain.

Notice that this gift was already resident inside Timothy. When the Lord plants His gift, it does not come and go but abides within. "For the gifts [*charisma*] and the calling of God are irrevocable" (Rom. 11:29). This gift, or power, is the equipment necessary to fulfill the call God places on each of us. Functioning in these gifts should be natural and comfortable for us. Just as the roles and functions of our individual parts don't vary or come and go, so it is with the gifts God imparts.

> ## Lifeless religion is born out of man's attempt to serve God his own way, in his own ability.

Paul wrote to the Roman believers, "I long to see you, that I may impart to you some spiritual gift [*charisma*], so that you may be established" (Rom. 1:11). The church will not be established without these gifts, the spiritual equipment that enables God's children to bring forth His will. Carefully read the following verse:

> As each one has received a gift [*charisma*], minister it to one another, as good stewards of the manifold grace of God.
> —1 Peter 4:10

We will examine three issues in this verse:

1. Everyone receives a gift.
2. The gift is not ours; we are merely stewards of it.
3. The gift is a portion of God's manifold grace.

1. Everyone receives a gift.

Notice it says, "As each one has received a gift, minister it." Peter did not say, "As the select few have received gifts." No, if you are born again and Spirit-filled, you have received God's gift to function in His body. There are no lame, useless parts in this body.

Paul says in Ephesians 4:7, "But to each one of us grace was given according to the measure of Christ's gift." And again in 1 Corinthians 7:7, "For I wish that all men were even as I myself. But each one has his own gift from God, one in this manner and another in that."

If we are ignorant of this we remain unable or unfit for service. Thus, our call goes unfulfilled. Just as babies learn to use their body parts, we must develop and exercise this gifting for service in His body. No part of His body operates outside of this supernatural ability.

2. The gift is not ours; we are merely stewards of it.

Since we do not own it, this gift is not to be neglected or used for personal gain. It is not ours to do with as we please. It is given that we might serve others. We are accountable for our care of it.

Paul was entrusted with a ministry of teaching and apostleship. He said, "I became a minister according to the gift of the grace of God given to me by the effective working of His power" (Eph. 3:7). Notice the importance he placed on being faithful to the gift:

> For if I preach the gospel, I have nothing to boast of, for necessity is laid upon me; yes, woe is me if I do not preach the gospel! For if I do this willingly, I have a reward; but if against my will, I have been entrusted with a stewardship.
>
> —1 Corinthians 9:16–17

Paul says, "Woe is me." Now *woe* is a very strong word. Jesus used it to warn of the pending judgment of certain individuals or cities. He said woe to

Chorazin and Bethsaida, cities that no longer exist (Matt. 11:21–22). He said woe to the scribes and Pharisees (Matt. 23), and to Judas (Matt. 26:24).

Woe is used by Jude to describe the judgment of evil men in the church. In the Book of Revelation it is used in reference to the inhabitants of the earth under God's judgment (Rev. 8:13). By using the word *woe,* Paul indicated the awesome responsibility of faithfulness to God's gift.

A Christian will backslide when he does not function in his gift or calling, just as a muscle atrophies with lack of use. An idle believer isolates himself, becoming easy prey for the enemy.

While studying the lives of great men and women of God, I found that those who fell had become idle or negligent in their call. Perhaps they were still ministering, but it was under the natural momentum achieved by their previous years of ministry. They began to use God's gift for their own benefit, not to protect and serve others.

King David fell into sin when he should have been at battle.

> It happened in the spring of the year, at the time when kings go out to battle, that

> David sent Joab and his servants with him,
> and all Israel; and they destroyed the peo-
> ple of Ammon and besieged Rabbah. But
> David remained at Jerusalem.
>
> —2 SAMUEL 11:1

David was king. God made him a king to shep-
herd and protect Israel. It was time for him to battle, not to stay home in Jerusalem enjoying the
rewards of past victories. He was relaxing, riding
on the benefits of his earlier labors. Bored, he
scanned his domain from the balcony and saw
Bathsheba bathing. The rest is history.

The point is, we are not here to take a vacation.
Our lives are not even our own—they were pur-
chased and given back to us for stewardship. We're
sojourners, not permanent residents. Too many
people act as if this life were their final destination!

Jesus said, "My food is to do the will of Him who
sent Me, and to finish His work" (John 4:34). This
should be our diet also. Jesus knew what was necessary to maintain His strength. Our strength is
drawn from food, both physical and spiritual. If we
cease to do His will, using His provisions for our
own benefit, we become weary and lose strength,

just as we would if we had stopped eating. With this loss of strength we find it easier to flow with this world, not against it. We become self-willed, self-centered, self-conscious and self-serving.

We have a great responsibility. We should not be people who go to church, apply nothing to our lives and become fat off the Word of God. God warns in Ezekiel 34:20, "Therefore thus says the Lord GOD to them: 'Behold, I Myself will judge between the fat and the lean sheep.'"

Who are the fat sheep? The ones who serve themselves with the good things of God to the neglect of others. Watch how God describes the fat sheep.

> Is it too little for you to have eaten up the good pasture, that you must tread down with your feet the residue of your pasture—and to have drunk of the clear waters, that you must foul the residue with your feet?... You have pushed with side and shoulder, butted all the weak ones with your horns, and scattered them abroad, therefore I will save My flock, and they shall no longer be a prey; and I will judge between sheep and sheep.
> —EZEKIEL 34:18, 21–22

God's gifts are not for our excess. God will test us with His goodness. We are to use the ability of God in our life to serve those who are weak, young or unable so that the body might be whole.

Don't misunderstand. It is right for us to enjoy the fruit of our labor. God gives us both rest and refreshing. But when our focus revolves around only ourselves, we become fat and careless. Gifts and talents used only to serve ourselves are not multiplied.

> God's gifts are not for our excess. God will test us with His goodness.

Each part of your body is accountable to the other parts. If your legs refused to work, your whole body would suffer. If your lungs or heart decided to stop, your other members would perish! If Satan can get us to focus on ourselves instead of serving others, then the entire body will suffer.

3. The gift is a portion of God's manifold grace.

The key word is *manifold,* or "many fold." Peter divides gifts into two major categories. The first is the oracle or speaking gift; the second, the ministry or serving gift. "If anyone speaks, let him speak as the oracles of God. If anyone ministers, let him do it as with the ability which God supplies" (1 Pet. 4:11).

Paul further divides these two categories. Look at this passage from the Book of Romans.

> For as we have many members in one body, but all the members do not have the same function, so we, being many, are one body in Christ, and individually members of one another. Having then gifts differing according to the grace that is given to us, let us use them: if prophecy, let us prophesy in proportion to our faith; or ministry, let us use it in our ministering; he who teaches, in teaching; he who exhorts, in exhortation; he who gives, with liberality; he who leads, with diligence; he who shows mercy, with cheerfulness.
>
> —Romans 12:4–8

Under the oracle category we find prophecy,

teaching, exhortation and leading; under the serving category are ministry (serving), giving and mercy.

Let me interject this point. You should not be in an oracle, or leader, position until you have proved faithful in serving one who is. There are many who want to lead and preach who have not laid their lives down to serve. No matter how talented they are, it is a disservice to both them and those under their care. If their character is not developed through serving, they will use their leadership position to lord it over people.

I have seen two extremes resulting from a lack of understanding. The first deals with those who think more highly of themselves than they ought. Mistaking the oracle for the only gift, they think it is the pinnacle of ministry and don't believe there is any other way to serve God.

This is incorrect. "For in fact the body is not one member but many...If the whole body were an eye, where would be the hearing? If the whole were hearing, where would be the smelling?" (1 Cor. 12:14, 17). They all want to be a mouth. Every part is important. Without the ministry of helps, the oracle ministry is limited. People try to move in a gift they *want* rather than the one they *have!*

The other extreme deals with those who believe ministry is limited to preachers or ministry staff. This mentality cripples the body, causing it to function at the level of an invalid.

Paul explains, "No, much rather, those members of the body which seem to be weaker are necessary. And those members of the body which we think to be less honorable, on these we bestow greater honor" (1 Cor. 12:22–23). This elevates the importance of the unnoticed. God made the unseen even more crucial than the seen. You can live without a voice but not without a liver or heart. Without these there would be no walking or talking.

The Book of Acts shows the attitude toward gifts in the early church. The early Christians realized there was much more to ministry than preaching, healing, deliverance and prophesying. Acts 6 mentions that some widows in the church of Jerusalem were neglected. They needed meals and help with other daily needs.

When this came to the attention of the leadership, they responded, "Therefore, brethren, seek out from among you seven men of good reputation, full of the Holy Spirit and wisdom, whom we may appoint over this business" (Acts 6:3). They found men who met these qualifications and brought them before the apostles. "When they had prayed, they laid hands on them. Then the word of God spread, and the number of the disciples multiplied greatly in Jerusalem" (vv. 6–7).

What happened when they laid hands on them? The gift to serve was imparted, and as a result, the word of God spread and disciples multiplied. These men operated in the gift that was given to them. What an amazing fact. Men serving widows caused the word of God to spread and the disciples to greatly multiply!

I believe one of the big reasons our churches are not growing and multiplying is because not all the people (congregations *and* leaders) are moving in their gifts. The Book of Acts even demonstrates how a leader who is operating in the gifts can bring a limited number of people to salvation, but when the whole church gets involved, the results are much greater.

Right after the Day of Pentecost, when Peter

preached, "that day about three thousand souls were *added* to them" (Acts 2:41, emphasis added; see also v. 47). Even when Peter walked the streets of Jerusalem under a healing anointing, "believers were increasingly *added* to the Lord, multitudes of both men and women" (Acts 5:14, emphasis added).

But when believers began to teach every day in every house (v. 42), then the church began "multiplying" (Acts 6:1). The next step was for believers to serve, which was begun with the ministry to widows. After that point, the church "multiplied greatly" (v. 7).

> # Revival is not just for the preachers but for the entire body—when every person takes his position.

Today pastors practically beg for volunteers. How sad. You don't see the leaders in the Book of Acts asking for volunteers. They took these serving positions so seriously that they searched out qualified men to wait tables—qualified on the basis of character, not talent. Then they were appointed. What importance they placed on something that today we consider trivial.

Responsibility to Be Faithful

What would happen if all believers functioned in their place? What tremendous things we would see. Revival is not just for the preachers but for the entire body—when every person takes his position.

Remember, the gift is the ability God gives us. We are not responsible for that which we were not entrusted with. The leg is not responsible for sight. Even so, the will of God can only be accomplished by the enabling of the Spirit. "Not that we are sufficient of ourselves to think of anything as being from ourselves, but our sufficiency is from God" (2 Cor. 3:5).

It is the joint operation of these gifts the enemy wants to stop. When successful he can severely hinder our growth—and cause us to feel powerless and without strength! He knows he cannot stop God from giving these gifts, so he is after our freedom to exercise them. Intimidation is the primary way he hinders this.

Don't allow him to steal your power. God has given you His gifts to enable you to be a powerful man or woman of God. Operate in the inner strength of His giftings, and become a "strong-man" for God.

Adapted from *Breaking Intimidation*, 43–53.

FIVE

Stir Up
Dormant Gifts

DEVELOPING
Inner Strength

On the very same day that Elijah turned a nation from its idols to the one true God, Ahab's wife, Jezebel, heard what was done to her prophets and sent a message to Elijah: "So let the gods do to me, and more also, if I do not make your life as the life of one of them by tomorrow about this time" (1 Kings 19:2). She was enraged with him, for those were her prophets, preaching her message. Now look at Elijah's response:

> And when he saw that, he arose and ran for his life, and went to Beersheba, which belongs to Judah, and left his servant there. But he himself went a day's journey into the wilderness, and came and sat down under a broom tree. And he prayed that he might die, and said, "It is enough! Now, LORD, take my life, for I am no better than my fathers!"
>
> —1 KINGS 19:3-4

The same day he won so great a battle, he ran for his life. He was so intimidated and discouraged by Jezebel that he wanted to die. The purpose of her intimidation was to prevent Elijah from completing God's purpose. She wanted to reverse his influence over the nation. She wanted him destroyed and out of the way. Even though she couldn't kill him, she still accomplished one goal by terrifying him into running away and wishing for death. Unwittingly, he was cooperating with her plan. If he could have seen clearer, he would have never run.

Every believer holds a position of authority that comes with God-given talents or gifts and is hidden in Christ Jesus above all demonic authority. So why are so many of us ineffective? To answer that, let's again read Paul's reminder to Timothy:

> Therefore I remind you to stir up the gift of God which is in you through the laying on of my hands.
>
> —2 Timothy 1:6

The Greek word for "stir up" is *anazopureo,* which means "to kindle afresh or keep in full flame" (Vine's dictionary). If Paul had to encourage this young man to stir up or kindle the gift *(charisma),* then it can become dormant! The gift does not work automatically. Like a fire it must be stirred up and kept going!

There are those with pure hearts and true intentions who believe that if God wants something to happen, it will just happen. But this is incorrect. Edmund Burke wrote in 1795, "The only thing necessary for the triumph of evil is for good men to do nothing "

Timothy was pure in heart. Remember how

Paul extolled his character? "For I have no one like-minded, who will sincerely care for your state. For all seek their own, not the things which are of Christ Jesus. But you know his proven character" (Phil. 2:20–21). Yet it is Paul who warned him twice not to neglect the gift of God, causing it to remain dormant.

So we need to answer this question: What causes the gift to become dormant?

The answer is in the following verse:

> Therefore I remind you to stir up the gift of God which is in you through the laying on of my hands. For [because] God has not given us a spirit of fear, but of power and of love and of a sound mind.
>
> —2 Timothy 1:6–7

The Greek word for fear is *deilia*. The word implies timidity and cowardice, and it is never used in a good sense in Scripture (Vine's dictionary). Look again at verse 7 from the New International Version:

> For God did not give us a spirit of timidity.
>
> —2 Timothy 1:7

The translators of the New International Version

believe *timidity* is the most accurate word for this verse, and so do I. Paul is telling Timothy, "Your gift of God is dormant because of timidity." Without changing the meaning, I could say:

> Timothy, the gift of God in you lies dormant because of intimidation!

Intimidated believers lose their authority in the spirit by default; consequently, their gift—God's ability in them—lies asleep and inactive. Though it is present, it is not in operation.

Intimidation wants to overwhelm you with a sense of inferiority and fear.

The objective of intimidation is to restrain you from action and coerce or force you into submission. Intimidation wants to overwhelm you with a sense of inferiority and fear. Once you've retreated into submission, either knowingly or unknowingly, you are a servant of the intimidator. You are no longer free to fulfill the will of God, but you are doomed to the desires of your intimidating captor.

Consequently, the gift of God, His spiritual ability in you, is inoperative. Now your authority has been stripped from you in order to be used against both you and those in your sphere of influence.

The origin of intimidation is fear, which has its root in our adversary, the devil. He is the originator of all fear and timidity (Gen. 3:1–10, especially v. 10). He will attack us by way of thoughts, imaginations and visions, or he will use circumstances and those under his influence to intimidate us. Either way, he has one objective: to control and limit us.

Elijah Intimidated?

The prophet Elijah operated in tremendous power. He stood boldly before a wicked king who had no fear of God and declared, "There shall not be dew nor rain these years, except at my word" (1 Kings 17:1). He was not afraid of this godless king.

He spent the next few years living in the miraculous. First, he was fed by ravens; then he was sustained by a widow whose meal and oil would not run out though famine and starvation were all around them. This widow's son suddenly died, and

God heard the prayer of Elijah, raising the boy from the dead. This was a man with a powerful ministry.

After a long period of time he again stood before the king. The king blamed Elijah for the hardship and suffering from the drought and greeted him with, "Is that you, O troubler of Israel?" (1 Kings 18:17).

Elijah boldly answered, "I have not troubled Israel, but you and your father's house have, in that you have forsaken the commandments of the LORD and followed the Baals" (v. 18). Then he commanded the king to gather up the 850 prophets of Baal and Asherah and take them to Mt. Carmel— along with the entire nation of Israel.

On the day of the confrontation all of Israel assembled to see who was the true God! Elijah boldly challenged the prophets of Baal and Asherah to offer a sacrifice to their gods at the same time he offered one to the Lord. "And the God who answers by fire, He is God," Elijah declared (v. 24).

The Lord God answered by fire, and the people of Israel fell on their faces and turned back to God. Then, under the orders of Elijah, they killed all 850 false prophets.

Next, Elijah proclaimed it would rain, earnestly praying and calling it forth when there was no sign of rain. In minutes the sky became black, and a heavy rain fell. As Ahab fled to his palace, the hand of God came upon Elijah, and he outran Ahab's chariot.

This was just one day in the life of Elijah. The nation turned around; the wicked were slain; the long drought was over. Elijah could clearly hear the voice of God, act on it and see great miracles.

> Intimidation will cause you to do things you never would do if you were not under its influence.

Symptoms of Intimidation

As we saw in our opening story about Queen Jezebel's intimidation of Elijah, an intimidating spirit unleashes confusion, discouragement and frustration. Its goal is to cause you to lose your proper perspective. Everything will seem overwhelming, difficult or even impossible. The stronger the intimidation, the greater the discouragement and hopelessness. If intimidation is not dealt with immediately, it will cause you to do things you never would do if you were not under its influence. This is exactly the goal of intimidation.

> When we are intimidated, we give up our position of authority. Consequently, the gift of God to serve and protect lies dormant.

"What Are You Doing Here?"

Elijah was knocked out of his authority when he did not confront Jezebel's intimidation head-on. As a result, his ministry gift to the nation was suppressed, and he went in a direction that was not God's desire. I'm sure he looked like quite a different man as he ran *away* from the confrontation he earlier ran *into*. He headed in the opposite direction, dropping off his servant and running forty days and nights to Mount Horeb.

Can you imagine? He is discouraged to the point of death, exhausted from running for forty days and in a state of depression. And God asks, "Why are you here?" Was God saying, "Why did you run from your post and hide here?"

You may be thinking, *Well, God sent the angel who gave Elijah the two cakes so he could run for forty days and nights. Why would God ask, "What are you doing here?"*

God knew Elijah was determined to run. When a man has it in his heart to do something, God will often let him do it even if it is not His perfect will.

When we are intimidated, we give up our position of authority. Consequently, the gift of God to serve and protect lies dormant. We end up unintentionally furthering the cause of the one intimidating us.

Adapted from *Breaking Intimidation*, 57–68.

Conclusion

God specializes in turning cowards into champions! Hallelujah! His power is perfected in weakness. "He who has begun a good work in you will complete it until the day of Jesus Christ" (Phil. 1:6). God turns our failures into victory! Don't draw back, but dare to believe the One who loved you and gave Himself for you.

God turns our failures into victory!

Let's pray together:

Father, in the name of Jesus I ask You to strengthen me through Your love and wisdom. Forgive me for drawing back in times of difficulty in order to preserve my own comfort and security. Lord Jesus, this day I choose to deny myself, take up my cross and follow You. I am Your servant; I receive Your grace that empowers so I might speak Your Word and perform Your will with all boldness and love. I will fulfill my destiny through the inner strength of Your might and power. In Jesus' name, amen.

If you are enjoying the Inner Strength Series by
John Bevere, here are some other titles from
Charisma House that we think will minister to you…

Breaking Intimidation
**Break free from the fear
of man**
John Bevere
ISBN: 0-88419-387-X
Retail Price: $13.99

The Bait of Satan
**Don't let resentment
cripple you**
John Bevere
ISBN: 0-88419-374-8
Price: $13.99

Thus Saith the Lord?
**How prophetic excesses
have hurt the church**
John Bevere
ISBN: 0-88419-575-9
Retail Price: $12.99

The Devil's Door
**Recognize the trap of
rebellion**
John Bevere
ISBN: 0-88419-442-6
Price: $12.99

Pathway to His Presence
**A 40-day devotional
leading into His presence**
John and Lisa Bevere
ISBN: 0-88419-654-2
Price: $16.99

The Fear of the Lord
**Gain a holy fear and awe
of God**
John Bevere
ISBN: 0-88419-486-8
Price: $12.99